SU

FLOURISH

A Guide to Wellbeing

Kev Bland

TURQUOISE
TIGER PRESS

Designed and edited by Turquoise Tiger Press, Lincolnshire, UK

Published by Kev Bland

Manufactured in the United Kingdom.

ISBN: 978-1-7398221-2-5

Preface

It's taken a few years to put this book together. I didn't realise writing it would reveal so many blind spots and forgotten memories. It has made me relive the past and implement every element of self-care documented in these pages.

I had no idea that I would learn so much about myself during the process, and I had no idea how much I would need to take my own advice, time and again, which we all know sucks.

My initial drafts were aimed solely at sharing the survive to flourish process with the guys on the Leg Up Project, a men's health group that I started as a result of the alarming rate of suicide in men.

There was a point, whilst writing, when it dawned on me how much my family and friends had suffered watching me go through the turmoil back then. It became apparent that it was fast becoming a cathartic exercise.

Throughout the process there have been enlightening moments, joy and laughter in recalling events, and more tears than I thought I had left to cry. I wasn't even sure if it would ever get finished, or if I had the confidence to share it. Turns out writing it was the easy bit!

But, if you are reading this then it got finished, and I mustered up the courage to be vulnerable and finally let it go.

For that I need to thank the ones who brought me joy in amongst the sadness, the very same who now give me the confidence and strength to share this.

Emily & Ella, I love you with all my heart.

To my brother Phil, who's been there throughout, where do I even begin?

Kev

Survive To Flourish

I lost my ID, my heart looked for someone to blame
I was torn into pieces, fragmented and shamed
Trapped in a torrent of confusion and rage
Understanding that nothing would quite be the same

But who was this new man held by walls firmly built?
A shadow of someone crippled by guilt
Where's forgiveness I ask? When I am to blame
As I punish myself again and again

This is madness in here, there's a struggle inside
Can I find some relief from this growing divide
In my head there's a fight and no can help
No one's coming to save me I must help myself

I find solace in silence, I walk 'til I'm beat
I take refuge in nature feel the earth on my feet
I submit to the fact that I'm just passing through

I let go of it all I just need to be true

So I look to the sun and the warmth that it brings
And I study the world to see where I fit in
I see beauty again as I start to grow
I awake from the dark where did all that time go?

I return to myself I am different but strong
I feel part of this now, I am loved, I belong.

Contents

Change Is the Only Constant

We've all been through the mill at one time or another, that's the way life is. Nobody gets away with it. Sometimes we blame everyone else for our misfortunes, but this doesn't serve us well. What we could be doing with that time is taking a good look at ourselves.

When I left the Marines over 20 years ago, I went missing for a little while. I lost my identity. I didn't know who I was anymore. I was injured, I got caught up in my own mind. I had little control over all the changes going on, and a very limited set of coping mechanisms—this all added to my scrambled head.

I guess deep down at the time, I didn't really like myself, I didn't like who I'd become. I made some bad decisions, I would face the consequences, and that's how it goes sometimes.

I know how hard it can be to pick yourself up when you're down and sometimes it feels like it's never gonna end. But it can all change if you want it to, and especially if you're willing to.

For me there was no quick fix, no one thing that changed, just a realisation that I needed to get myself out of the dark place I'd ended up in and the only way was to start making better decisions. I became accountable for my actions, I took ownership of my life, I stopped blaming everyone else.

Let's not forget that we all have difficulties to overcome. Problems are a fact of life, but if we can look at them as a challenge, or as a learning opportunity, they become easier to resolve or we can at least take something positive from the experience. Perception is everything; mindset can be changed.

And knowing this is the right place to start.

Greek philosopher Heraclitus is quoted as saying "change is the only constant in life." And that sounds obvious, but that doesn't mean we should just sit back and wait for change to happen to us.

It's a given that we 're all going to have to deal with loss at some time in our life, and I know how that feels, I know that's not easy.

The past can bring regret, but we can change our perspective and try to find positive new meaning to past traumas. The uncertainty of the future can weigh heavy, however that's not happened yet so let's just focus on the now and deal with the evidence in front of us.

Let's concentrate on our ability to control the controllable in our life, let's accept where we are and move forward. Let's choose to be proactive. Let's train hard and fight easy, as we used to say in the Marines.

Grow From Discomfort

Staying on top of things is a daily task for us all, but without taking time to reflect, we never get a chance to realise how strong we've been—or how tough we are.

I'm sharing the most important aspects of what I've learned on my journey so far. However simple some may seem, they helped me to create a positive outlook and make better choices when under pressure. Don't overlook the basics; if we get them right, it can make a huge difference.

I'm not saying I've got it all sorted now, we all know that's not how it works. But we do have to accept there's more hardship on its way. Let's not be defeated by this, we know shit happens.

We grow from discomfort and if we choose to challenge ourselves on a regular basis, we are better prepared for life's setbacks.

The thought of writing a journal, a poem, or just making notes on your feelings might make you feel uncomfortable. But these exercises are invaluable to increase self-awareness, they may help you find clarity in a situation, and even find meaning in past trauma.

Since I can remember I've always written. I enjoy putting the words together in a poem, and capturing my thoughts helps me to gain clarity. I get a sense of fulfilment, it's cathartic, and writing tends to highlight the important stuff that's going on in my life. It feels odd at times because I get to delve into old memories and ways of thinking. Some of it's funny, some makes me cringe, and some of it is still a little bit upsetting to read.

I'd written some very dark poetry and songs when I was injured and still in the Marines, I hadn't realised how dark until I re-read them years later.

Being injured sucked. I borrowed my brother's guitar and started to play. I went on to write songs, join a band, and share my thoughts and feelings as I went out gigging for a few years. I guess I just wanted to be understood. I think we all need to feel heard when we feel uncertain in our lives. What later dawned on me was that I needed to understand who I was first.

It had been a relatively private affair between me and my notebooks, with only a handful of trusted friends let into that side of my life. But entering a speaking competition with the Professional Speaking Association (PSA) would change all that. A huge thanks to Adam Harris for inviting me in to the speaking world.

After working through lots of ideas relating to men's mental health, I came up with a concept that excited me. If I could meet myself on the day I left the Marines, what would I say?

That five-minute talk would be a reflective piece, one that would take me well out of my comfort zone and reveal a few demons.

I stumbled across answers to questions I hadn't even thought of yet, and ultimately, it led me to write this book.

Maybe you should think about what makes you feel uncomfortable, maybe there's something you would like to do but it scares you a bit. Just think of it as preparation for future hardship and a chance to learn something new about yourself.

Talking To Myself

If you could have five minutes to give your past self some advice, what would you say?

I was excited about the concept of my talk, and the fact that I was entering a speaking competition. I'd never done that before and I was feeling the pressure. Hey, we grow from discomfort!

Anyway, giving myself a 'heads up' on the next 20 years fascinated me. What would I say, especially as I only had five minutes, five minutes to have a word with my past self?

I remember the idiot that left the Marines. This was going to be interesting.

I spent weeks and weeks working on what to say, choosing which bits of advice not to use was also difficult. It took a lot of time to drill it back down to those five minutes.

A few months later and there I was. I'd done the prep and then I was called onto the stage, ready to be judged by a panel of three expert speakers. Here we go!

At around three minutes in my tongue was sticking to the side of my mouth, the only glass of water I could see was on the table in front of me, it was one of the judges'.

My eyes flicked between the judge and his glass. I looked at him, I was still talking. My mouth was so dry, so I just picked his glass up, emptied it and put it straight back down. I looked at him and whispered "sorry". I'd got this, shit, what am I doing look on my face.

But that was it. Another 120 seconds later it was all done. I thought well, that could have been worse. I sat back down, looked at my watch and my heart rate monitor read 140 beats per minute. I couldn't believe it!

And yeah, just in case you're wondering, I didn't win, but the experience was amazing! I came third and won a book, so I was quite pleased with that.

I apologised to judge, Simon Hazeldine, for necking his glass of water in front of everyone, he was an absolute gent about it.

More importantly, I'd put myself well out of my comfort zone, grown from the experience and, without realising at the time, it was a pivotal moment in my life.

I'd created a system to improve wellbeing and I wasn't fully aware of how important that would be.

Evolve or Die

As Marines we were trained to suppress emotion, and to advance towards danger as part of a 'well-oiled machine'. We trained hard and learned that we needed to be able to rely on one another when situations become tough. Without this culture, specialised teams cannot complete seemingly unachievable tasks. With such strong back up in place we can achieve the impossible—well, maybe the unthinkable.

I now see that love and belonging, and a strong sense of purpose are what underpin our ability to do great things in our life. Along with this, constant change requires us to be able to adapt to situations as they happen, so the faster we can adjust, the better our chances of survival. In simple terms: evolve or die.

I'd left the Marines in a state I refer to as survival mode; I was not in a good place. I lacked the experience to adapt quickly to my new life. I'd left injured without realising how much I used physical exercise to regulate stress, I just took that for granted. I was angry, I was uncertain, and I was frustrated. I found myself on a steep learning curve taking a lot of risks. Drinking and taking drugs. I was all over the place! I hadn't developed the skills to deal with my new life. Drinking was my go-to coping mechanism, but it doesn't work, it creates more problems.

Looking back now I know that I had a distinct lack of emotional self-awareness. I couldn't recognize subtle emotions in people, I was brash, I'd steam roller through any problems that came up. It affected my relationships and made hard work of everything.

During this massive transition in my life, I was wrestling with a whole new set of feelings that I didn't understand. It was difficult. I would later realise that my emotions were just trying to redirect me to make better decisions and take positive action—I'd been suppressing them for far too long.

The problem was, I didn't understand what the emotions were telling me; I was running on instinct without reasoning.

Change the Way You Think

Our instinct to survive is the most powerful drive we have. Our evolution has been guided by this essential purpose. It affects the way we think, how we feel, how we act, and how we communicate.

I may have left the Marines, but my head hadn't. I was still on high alert; hyper-vigilant and looking for 'the threat' 24/7. And when you look for trouble, you tend to find it; that's what happened to me.

When we talk about survival instincts, most people think of the fight, flight and freeze responses to stress: Many of us will have experienced these to some degree in our lives.

We must not judge others based upon how we process our feelings because we all experience emotions differently.

Fight, flight and freeze are the most obvious physical responses to immediate danger, but there's also the psychological impact to consider. Surviving to fight was what Marine training had prepared me for—that's surviving to fight—not fighting to survive! But that wouldn't help me with the more emotional problems I was dealing with. Fatherhood, finding work, fixing broken relationships.

I was in new territory. It was written all over my face, and I wasn't even aware of it. I said things that upset people when I was trying to make them laugh, and I made people laugh when I was being serious – I just wasn't getting it!

I would though, eventually, but it would take a lot of heartbreak to get there.

The behaviour cycle is a concept that links our attitude and behaviour. We must accept responsibility for our actions and the way we choose to think. We can change both with some effort.

My attitude affects my behaviour – my behaviour affects your attitude – your attitude affects your behaviour — and then your behaviour affects my attitude.

Our attitude is driven by our mindset, which is the way that we think or perceive certain situations to be. It affects our behaviour because it prompts our actions. What we think is our reality; remember we all think differently.

Our behaviour then affects everyone else's attitude towards us, and in turn this prompts their behaviour to us. Don't forget that words spoken and actions taken cannot be undone.

So how does this help? Well, it all boils down to our self-awareness. We can take an honest look at our own attitude and appreciate how it impacts on our behaviour. Let's not forget our attitude depicts how others treat us also.

Have a listen to the voice in your head, your internal dialogue. What are your beliefs? Do you think well of others? Are you being kind to yourself? How is your mind set? And are you open to change?

Let's consider empathy too, because we don't know what everyone else is dealing with, we don't know what everyone else is going through.

Taking this perspective made it easy for me when dealing with conflicting views. I got to a point in my life where I'd accept that I would never truly know what that other person was dealing with, and I'd try to be more understanding to break a negative cycle. It took time to reprogramme the way I thought, but it made my life far less stressful.

Are you letting your past define your present? Are you looking for trouble without realising it and creating more problems for yourself, more than you're solving?

Do you need to change the way you think?

Monkey Mind

Let's delve into fight, flight and freeze.

For me, fight is less about having a scrap with somebody, and more about our internal dialogue, that voice in our head, the one we wrestle with when we're going through indecision.

Sometimes there's so much going on in our lives we struggle to rest our minds and this is the real fight for many of us. This was the fight for me.

When I started Tai Chi, I heard this state of mind being described as Monkey Mind. In his best-selling book, The Chimp Paradox, Professor Steve Peters refers to the 'inner chimp', as that part of our instinct that makes survival our number one priority, sidestepping our rational thought process.

The 'chimp' can help us when under immediate threat but can hinder us in complex interpersonal situations.

Every one of us, to some degree, is in a constant internal dialogue. This 'self-talk', it's not us going mad, we are influenced by our subconscious mind; it reveals our thoughts and beliefs about how we fit in to the world outside.

If we are not fulfilled in our lives, the way we talk to ourselves is often negative, reinforcing self-doubt and lowering our self-esteem. To stand any chance of finding personal success, or happiness, we need to ensure this internal dialogue works for us in a positive way, and that begins by becoming aware of it. I mentioned earlier that I write, and this is where I started to explore my inner chimp.

The same goes for flight. It's not as simple anymore, it's not as simple as running from a sabre tooth tiger, like in days of old. We 'run away' from so many of our problems by avoiding them, usually the ones that require a tough decision to be made.

For some situations, I think that inaction can work to our advantage. I used to say, "if in doubt, do nothing", but I took this to the next level and avoided making timely decisions that really needed to be made.

It's good practice to stop and take a breath, maybe pause awhile. But again, there comes a time when we must choose a path to take before a decision is made for us.

Freezing is our instinct to play dead and wait for the danger to pass, or nowadays maybe we just want to blend in and lower the chances of getting singled out. Social disapproval is something we instinctively want to avoid, social media has forever changed the way we see ourselves. It's complicated.

Sadly, freezing is common among young children in abusive situations, whether at home or being bullied at school. They freeze because they're just unable to fight back or run away.

About bullying, it's not just reserved for outside the school gates, it's prevalent throughout our whole lives, with corporate bullying another serious issue these days.

This book aims to help you become more assertive and take greater control of your life. Some decisions are harder than others; but ultimately decisions must be made.

Listen to how you speak to yourself, have you been kind in your mind? Are you being nice to yourself and others?

Is your monkey in check?

Let me ask you a question, who is in control of your life? For the most part, that is. You or the chimp?

Emotionally Hijacked

Fortunately, I'd studied Daniel Goleman's work on emotional intelligence not long after leaving the marines. His concept of emotional hijacking changed the way I think forever. It made me realise that I could step up to a different level of self-regulation. Knowing that I could control my anger and rage better by practising breathing techniques made a massive difference. I was less anxious, I started to listen to people more, I had more empathy for others, and I felt more in control of my actions.

In simple terms, emotional hijacking occurs when we are emotionally triggered, the red mist appears, and we lose control. Cortisol, our primary stress hormone, initiates a surge of energy to ready us for action.

It takes training and practice to maintain clarity when this happens to us. Whilst delivering a workshop at one of Her Majesty's prisons, I had the opportunity to address a group of around 40 inmates. Like myself, many of them were veterans.

The lads talked about the 'split second' decisions they had made, the regret they carried, and a wish that they had been able to control their emotions and actions better. That evening I realised just how close I had been to joining them at one point in my life.

Outside of interpersonal relationships, the most likely place that you will experience getting emotionally hijacked is on our busy roads. Research in 2018, from leading transport website Fleet News, suggests that one in five drivers experience road rage at least once a week, with 18 to 24-year-olds being the group most affected. There's a whopping 42% of that age group admitting that they get angry whilst driving every single day. That's a serious issue and begs the question, is there a need to make young drivers aware of the dangers and consequences of emotional hijacking?

If you find yourself in an altercation with another driver, you can reduce the chance of being emotionally hijacked. Stay in the car and buy yourself a bit of thinking time by taking a few deep breaths, this will bring some clarity. Try not to take or make the issue personal, because let's be honest, it's doubtful anyone had the intention to mess up in the first place.

If we were all a bit more self-aware, and able to think a little before we said or did something we would later regret, the world would be a much nicer place. Who knows, without this knowledge all those years ago, my life may have turned out to be very different.

If this resonates with you, and you want to feel more in control, get yourself a copy of Goleman's book, Emotional Intelligence: Why it can matter more than IQ.

Are You Ok?

Clinical Psychologist Dr Reisinger, of Zucker Hillside Hospital in New York, believes that the fight, flight, freeze model oversimplifies our responses to stress; he expands on it to add flood, fawn, and fatigue.

Reisinger's work forced me to revise my notes, it struck a huge chord with me.

Flood, fawn and fatigue are less likely to be associated with our survival responses, but they are becoming more prevalent with modern day pressures. They trigger the same physiological responses we get with fight, flight and freeze.

Flooding can be described as the inability to control our emotions, and like all the responses in the survival mode model, it's normal when there's a lot to process emotionally.

It can happen in response to misunderstanding, to grief, conflict, or to any other situation that overwhelms us. We do not tend to reason or listen properly when we are flooded. Supressed emotions can also be triggered sub consciously, so sometimes we have no idea why we feel so overwhelmed.

Flooding becomes problematic when it continues over long periods of time. Unless we learn to understand, overcome or change the way we feel about past or present events, we may never reach our full potential to manage our feelings.

This can get even more complicated when we're dealing with multiple issues, and then we struggle to unravel what is at the heart of the problem.

My injury meant that I couldn't train to alleviate anxiety and anger, and I was using negative coping mechanisms to numb out the dark thoughts. I pushed everyone away who loved me because I didn't have the courage to share what was going on in my head.

I wasn't looking after myself properly, I didn't trust anyone in my immediate circle, I had no balanced understanding of my own feelings, and I didn't have the headspace to understand anybody else's either.

When I was flooded I 'd be laughing one minute and crying the next. I could just about hold myself together at work, but that was difficult. I'd get home from work, out of sight of everyone, and it just came bursting out. I think a lot of us go through that.

So, if you've never heard of the term 'flooded', but you can identify with my experience, don't think that you can't change this, and know that you are not alone in feeling this way.

I eventually shared my thoughts when I started to work with a music producer. He became a trusted friend who also spurred me on to write this book. Thanks, Nick, for being there, listening without judging, and for taking the piss when I needed it most, like that time somebody fire-bombed my garage on my birthday! Anyway, I digress.

Catastrophic thinking, or ruminating on irrational thoughts, will stop us from taking positive action and add to our anxiety. It can also be the lead up to taking your own life.

If you feel flooded right now, dig deep and find the courage to ‘open up’, talk to someone you trust, or book an appointment to see the GP.

It’s at our darkest times when we learn the most about who we are, let it pass and start afresh.

Giving Up and Shutting Down

For me, the fawn response is that feeling where you have lost all motivation, you struggle to find clarity in making your own decisions, and you tend to become a people pleaser constantly looking for validation to feel ok.

That's a place I've been to, a deep feeling of uncertainty in all you say and do. A shitty way to exist in a world of low self-esteem.

I gave up, I was tired out. I didn't answer the door to anyone, I didn't open mail for months at a time. I'd lost all hope and the bailiffs paid me a visit, but that was the least of the problems in my head. I was really struggling.

If you're feeling this way, know that it will pass when you muster the courage to ask for help.

These feelings are a trigger to take positive action. I totally missed the signpost for fawn and sauntered slowly into Fatigue.

Fatigue is common these days. It may be from exam stresses at school, college or university. Your working environment also plays a huge part in your overall health, however, I would take a good look at the people you surround yourself with if you are running on empty all the time.

Every interpersonal relationship you have in your life will impact positively or negatively. What we take from each interaction is up to us. Only we have the ability to change ourselves.

The mind and body are inextricably linked, and in extreme cases mental fatigue will literally take your body down, you will become physically unwell. Chest pains, shortness of breath or panic attacks are very real symptoms of health anxiety, fatigue clouds the mind, so it's important to be aware of the warning signs.

If you feel every day is a bad day; you have no interest in anything that you do; you have no time for people; you feel hopeless and overwhelmed; and you're exhausted all the time, you need to seek help.

And if you're taking unnecessary risks, or using drugs and alcohol to get through the day, it's time to stop and consider the consequences.

Think of it this way; you are telling yourself that your life needs to change. You may not know what to do, or feel capable of making any decisions, but you will need to seek help.

Do not forget that there is a route back to good mental health, that these feelings will pass if you are willing to do the hard work.

Act, don't hide, talk to a GP if this is where you are right now.

Drink, Drugs and Drama

Negative past experiences flooded back and collided with the current shit storm I was in. I'd caused it, I had nothing good to report about my behaviour. It was unacceptable. I was angry with who I had become and the situation that I'd found myself in, and at the time I couldn't see a way out.

My go to coping mechanisms didn't help; drinking and taking drugs just led to more drama. The three d's of doom!

The panic attacks, anxiety, and pains in my chest made me feel like I was dying. Family break ups and missing my kids hit me hard.

And like I said, eventually I went to my doctor and told her how I felt: stupidly happy one minute, sobbing the next, angry, frustrated, and hopelessly lost. This had been going on for months. I was masking it at work and on the outside I appeared okay to most.

It helped to talk to trusted friends and colleagues. I cut right down on the three d's of doom. Drinking alcohol went first and that was a game changer. I read countless self-help books, and, little by little, I started to take control of my life and get my agency back.

Unravelling my feelings and thoughts was slow, but beginning that process was absolutely crucial if I ever wanted to be happy again. Positive change really started to happen when I finally decided to take up tai chi classes. It was tough to walk into the first session, but I'm glad that I did. Learning to breathe properly and to meditate is what would set me on the path to better health.

I meditated to get to sleep. It took lots of practise before I started to feel the benefit, but I sussed it out. I still had good and bad days but, as the good outweighed the bad, my life started to improve, and I felt lighter, I started to get a spring back in my step.

My situation, at the time, was not one I could just walk away from, but it was emotional space that I needed to find, and tai chi worked for me. The breathing, the meditating.

We can't be happy and have a meaningful existence living in survival mode all the time, we need to take positive action and learn to flourish in our lives.

Looking back at the dark times I faced feels odd now, it's almost like it wasn't me that felt such lows and uncertainty. The grief, the guilt, the self-loathing all started as I began to realise my part in everything. I can't believe how long it lasted and how long it took me to work through the fog in my head. Is it strange to think that I wish the older me could have somehow been there to guide me? I guess that sharing my journey, to help others, is a way of making those tough lessons seem worthwhile.

I blame the chimp! But seriously, I look at hardship as necessary growing pains that help us become more aware of who we are and more responsible for our actions.

That first step is the hardest, but it's one that needs to be taken soonest.

Act, Don't Hide

We need our survival instincts to be in place so that, if needed, they will kick in and, hopefully, assist us in seeing another day, but by understanding ourselves better, we can self-regulate and function with more control over our emotions. I believe the key is not to suppress them, but to learn to process them in a positive way.

'Diving' straight into past traumas to analyse and unravel what you could have done differently is not at all helpful, although I have done that myself. Positive action will always be the starting point because you can't think your way out of a problem without taking some form of action.

If you begin by accepting where you are and deciding where you want to be, you can start to gain some level of control back. Easy to say and hard to do, I know, but what other options are there?

You may be experiencing grief, it's more common than you think. We grieve over loss of identity when something significant changes in our life. This may also trigger grief through loss of safety which can happen from divorce, eviction, being cheated on or past trauma.

Lost dreams or expectations cause us to grieve, as does loss of autonomy, the ability to manage our own lives. Injury, financial difficulties, illness, losing our eyesight, our hair, our health, all these things can bring on grief. It's a very human thing to experience.

Acceptance is the last stage of grief, and you must allow yourself to grieve, there's no time limit, we are all different. However, coming to terms with your 'new' reality will be the beginning of a return to feeling human again.

Identifying the positive aspects that you have learned from past trauma can help you figure out a way to move forward. What did I learn? Patience, humility, honesty, empathy, to name a few.

Experiencing life in survival mode is mentally draining. Having a healthy mind must be the number one priority. Allowing yourself to let go of previous thought processes is not easy, it's uncomfortable and challenging, but we don't need to make more mistakes to learn, even though we will, just not the same ones, hopefully.

We also need to learn to fail. Everybody fails, it's part of life, so learn to be ok with it.

We need to accept uncertainty as the norm, because life is uncertain, and we need to know that growth only occurs through discomfort. It's all part of the process.

I can't undo the emotional trauma felt by my loved ones when I was unwell, but my reconciliation came with forgiving myself and becoming a better person, sharing my time more and supporting those that need a leg up too.

We simply must do whatever we can to move our lives forward in a positive direction, and understand that above all, we are only human. We will make mistakes, we will fail at times, but ultimately, we must always strive to become better, whatever setbacks we experience.

Be good to yourself. Forgive yourself, accept your current situation, and move forward.

Become better, not bitter.

We are all work in progress, the hardship is part of the process.

House of Mirrors

I got injured in the Marines after exiting a helicopter and landing badly. It was the beginning of the end for my career, but I was yet to find that out.

It took me almost a year to get an x-ray. I'd been on high doses of pain killers throughout that time and spent months in a fighting unit. I thought the meds were fucking me up so I stopped taking them, the pain got worse and the medical officer ripped into me when I went to see him. I basically 'refused to soldier' until I got it looked at. I was booked in to Derriford Hospital, Plymouth, the next day.

I found out that my shin was broken near my knee, and it had caused further injury to my tendons. I broke down when I saw the x-ray, I was beginning to think it was all in my head.

I wanted to apply for special forces selection and join the Special Boat Service. I'd passed out of training as the Kingsbadgeman, the best overall recruit, and the training team had taken me to one side to point me in that direction, so at the time it was looking achievable. But the injury, or the drugs, had literally crushed my spirit. I was devastated.

I struggled to maintain a sense of belonging, no one wanted a broken Marine in their troop, and I felt surplus to requirement.

I had always written poetry and leant on my pen more than ever to find an escape and a way to organise my thoughts.

As the years passed, I would revisit my notebooks full of poetry and songs, they helped me to see how far I've truly come in terms of my outlook on life. I didn't expect to be using them as a reference to write a book, but here we are.

The fog of who I had been hung around for many years. I had lost my identity. I'm not saying that I didn't have any fun, far from it. But in the time I spent alone, I felt disconnected, unsure, and often angry. Uncertainty with no idea of what I wanted from life had become my norm. I was living in survival mode worrying about the things I had no control over.

I've only recently learned, through research whilst writing this book, that the painkillers I had been on had serious side effects. I felt angry when I found out. Maybe things would have been different? Maybe I wouldn't have been such a dickhead?

Co-proximal was banned in 2009 for good reason: two of its common side effects are listed as hallucinations and visual disturbances. I was experiencing some of this and, at the time, I didn't have the courage to share that with anyone.

This new insight helped me to understand my behaviour back then. I'd lost my sense of agency; I'd lost control of my life. It was like being in a house of mirrors and wondering who the guy in the reflection was.

Another side effect was a general feeling of physical weakness; not something that would benefit anyone serving in a fighting company of Marines.

As expected, the Marines is a harsh environment to be in, but I'd become used to it; we become our environment. I was deep in survival mode at the end of my career. I wasn't likely to take advice from anyone, I didn't either. I thought I knew best, and I would end up leaving just to get away.

This was a bad idea, and one that I will never repeat again. Fail to plan, plan to fail. Yep, there's a lesson in itself!

Absent Without Leave

The tough decisions in life that we have to make define who we are, what we truly value, and what we stand for.

Being turfed out of a fighting unit was bad enough, but after months in plaster at home on sick leave I was posted to driver training school, and on to the logistics regiment. This was never part of my plan. I arrived at my new unit and was hugely underwhelmed to meet my Sergeant, a man who enjoyed his rank in the worst possible way. I was still trying to recover physically but my head would be playing catch up for many more years to come. Being on 'light duties' meant no deployments, no physical training, no ceremonial duties, and no fucking self-esteem.

I was in a long-term relationship and, after a few months of being there, my girlfriend fell pregnant. When she was due to give birth, I went to see the Sergeant to ask for leave. When he found out I wasn't married he smugly laughed and said, 'well you're not going anywhere then'.

Before I'd even left his office, I'd made my decision. I went back to the accommodation, packed my kit and off I went to see my first child being born. Our relationship hadn't been strong. I'd been a nightmare to be around for some time and the next two weeks would be a blur of mixed emotions. The birth was difficult and we nearly lost her. It was traumatic and I stayed home as long as I dared. I didn't really want to go back, but I'd already been 10 days absent without leave and it was time to face the music.

The journey back to camp was the hardest 240 miles I'd ever driven, plenty of time to wonder what would happen to me. It hadn't been that long since I marched up to take the Kingsbadge. And now I was AWOL, I was injured, and I was a father. I just wasn't fucking ready for any of it.

As I was driving up to the camp gates, the gravity of what I'd done, and the anxiety, started to hit me. Just before I reached the barrier I looked left and there, in all its glory, was the church. I drove into the carpark, got out of the car and went to see the Padre. I have no recollection of the discussion and I can't remember what happened over the next few weeks. I hesitantly went back to my unit and kept a low profile and nothing was said about my unauthorised absence.

I can only assume that the sergeant had received a massive bollocking for his part in it. I'll never know for sure, but I did remain on the top of his shit list for the rest of my time there. That basically meant if there were any 'gash' jobs needed to be done I was his number one man.

I eventually took a medical discharge. It was a sad way to leave such a big part of my life.

I felt like I'd failed, I felt ashamed, and I guess that feeling of love and belonging that I had been part of is just about impossible to match. So much had changed for me, I struggled to adjust and our relationship broke down before I left the Corps.

As we do though, I cracked on, but it wasn't until about 15 years later that I would start to rebuild my Royal Marine network and reconnect with some old faces.

Social media has made this easy to do, but like many veterans, I was very uneasy about letting the world know where I was. Past active service plays a huge role in the paranoia that most veterans experience. It's ingrained in you to constantly be on the lookout for the 'threat', but that mindset can stop you from flourishing if you don't keep it in check.

After 10 years of teaching in education, the paranoia had faded and I was ready for a new challenge. You may think that's a long time, however, in the middle of all that I received a letter from the MOD stating that my records had gone missing after a laptop had been stolen in Birmingham. Great, I spent time in Northern Ireland and that news wobbled me a fair bit. I eventually left education and went on to dabble in the film industry by doing some specialist background work.

When we are at a low ebb, we see things differently. I felt backed into a corner and went AWOL, I ran from the situation. I could have gone to the Padre on the way out of the camp gates, not on the way back in. But no regrets on that one.

By the true nature of displaying courage, we are left feeling vulnerable, uncomfortable, and exposed, but hiding from problems can lead to a life of regret.

What we should be aiming for is finding the courage to ask the right questions to the right person, at the right time.

Let me make my message clear, have the courage of your convictions.

Good Intentions

I'd left the Marines and I was trying to replace the excitement and camaraderie that I once had. I'd also met somebody new and tried to settle into my new life over the next few years.

Playing guitar and singing in a band gave me a great excuse to do what I wanted, and to say what I wanted through the music that we wrote and performed. It was good for me. I created a new persona and I vented. I needed to let some pressure out, I think I just wanted to be understood.

Writing songs was a big part of my journey then. Self-exploration and soul searching uncovered painful truths, and accepting the poor decisions I made along the way was part of the process. Growing pains.

It had felt good to be in a band. It was good fun and a massive release, but relationships would become strained as I delved into my head and struggled to address the crumbling situation at home. I just didn't know what to do, it was complicated and the more I tried to work it out, the more confused I became.

Things steadily went downhill; I'd lost so much weight from anxiety; I'd lost one third of my body weight since leaving the Marines.

The jobs I managed to hold down got worse as my self-worth faded. At one stage I was delivering sandwiches from a van for £3.50 an hour whilst running a music studio at night.

I'd set the studio up with the few grand compensation I received for my injury. It was totally on impulse without any thought as to how it would work out. We were skint, but I was foolishly confident and, with no idea of how to run a business, I ended up getting into serious debt and almost lost the house. I was creating more problems than I was solving.

Living hand to mouth, taking chances and having no clear plan, it couldn't go on for long and, looking back, it was always going to pile in.

I'd become a father again, but my partner was suffering with post-natal depression. I didn't even know it existed, I didn't know what it was. We were both dealing with poor mental health and a so-called friend had slowly been driving a wedge between us.

We had a beautiful daughter together but our trust for one another was broken in amongst the confusion and we separated. Coming out of that relationship would be the toughest part of my whole life. I was heartbroken.

I remember looking at myself in the bathroom mirror not long after we'd split up. I'd shaved my head. I'd do it on impulse when things got a bit too much for me. I think it was like a reset, maybe a visual reminder to start afresh, like going back to being a recruit where all the nervous energy was directed towards moving forward.

I was sobbing, I was angry, and sick of this disconnected feeling that I couldn't begin to describe.

I asked the guy in the mirror, out of desperation "where's that fucking Marine when I need him?"

It was a wakeup call, and, without a doubt, it was my children that gave me a reason to change. They made me realise I'd got to sort myself out if I was ever going to be the father I promised myself I could be.

A lifelong friend, with a cracking sense of humour, would be instrumental in helping me to get back into proper work and raise my spirits. He'd seen me at my best, and it must have been painful for him to see me at my worst. He dropped in on me one day to see how I was and suggested I go electrical contracting with him.

Before joining the Marines I'd served with the RAF as an aircraft electrical technician. I had qualifications, but no experience on site, and my confidence was at an all-time low.

I laughed at him and explained my fears. He laughed back and said, 'come on mate, you'll piss it, what's the worst that can happen?'

There were loads of guys on site less able than me, just winging their way through it, trying to earn a living. This built my confidence up and it didn't take long to start feeling ok about my ability.

Being a sub-contractor wasn't what I wanted to do but It raised my self-esteem, and it raised my bank balance. This was the start of me taking more responsibility for my own actions, accepting the position I was in, and I guess, growing up a little bit too.

Accepting help can be one of the hardest things to do. The deeper into survival mode we get the harder it seems to be to ask for help.

Friendships based on authentic intent do not happen by chance, we must cultivate them. They need to be mutual, no filters, no bullshit.

We need people in our lives who accept our faults, without judgement, but still tell us when we are being unreasonable.

We also need to be that friend to ourselves and others too.

Living on Purpose

I'd been on self-destruct for several years and I was exhausted, but I'd pick myself up and dust myself off time and again, I kept going. I kept going to tai chi, I was keeping my chimp in order, for the most part. I had the odd blow out, you know how it is.

But I was doing better things, I was thinking positively for more of the time and helping others out, and it felt good. It felt like the right thing to do. And that's where an opportunity 'sprung up' for me.

I left the subbie role and stepped into a teaching job feeling a bit like a fraud again, a feeling that some refer to as imposter syndrome. There was self-doubt, and apprehension, the usual anxiety we feel when we step out of our comfort zone, and I'd done that plenty of times.

The contract work had become tedious, finding new work all the time drained me. I'd quite often turn up and get laid off with no notice. There's a lot of pressure in the construction industry. ONS data from 2020 reveals that the suicide rate for construction workers is more than 3 times the national average.

I thought this new role could be my turning point, and because I'd had enough of construction it was a no brainer for me to give it a go. It would be the role that would bring me back to life.

My initial brief was basic - get the learners to attend. My class of year 10 and 11s had all been removed from mainstream education for behavioural issues and the college was struggling to find a suitable tutor to get them to turn up and stay in lessons. Numerous teachers before me hadn't lasted any longer than a few weeks with this 'high spirited' group of young teenagers.

The senior managers had little expectations for them. This took the pressure off me, and I was left to manage it with very little input from above.

I drew upon my experience as a Marine, as I didn't have any formal teaching experience or qualifications yet. Having said that, I had taught as a cadet for a few years, and I'd stepped into several instructional roles in the military too, so strangely enough we do have transferrable skills, even if we don't 'badge them up' with the same name.

I was harsh, but fair, I treated them with honesty and respect, and, even though they were a handful, they responded well.

It had been five years since I'd left the corps. I hadn't realised what important things were missing from my life - a sense of purpose and a feeling of belonging. I was good at teaching and my heart was in it. I loved it, it came naturally to me and that would be the start of my professional self-reflective journey.

I got through the initial anxiety within a few months, because we do, and I settled in. It was demanding, but it took my mind off all the uncertainty of what was going on in my personal life. Before this job I wasn't sure whether it had been my relationship or the work, but between the two I hadn't been happy.

It was weird, but this job gave me an opportunity to be present and immerse myself. I let all the other shit sort itself out and concentrated on work.

I flourished at the college and, after a few years, was invited to join the quality audit and teacher training teams. These new insights became a double-edged sword. The more I learnt about how our education system worked, the less I believed that it did.

Although I could make a greater difference in those teams, I was constantly banging heads with the senior managers. I firmly believe in focusing on learner and staff wellbeing to raise standards and achievement; but the culture at the time there just didn't see it that way. Maybe it was time to move on?

The politics, the cutbacks, the pressure from above, it was just impossible for me to bring, what I believed, to be quality to that role.

With my daughters getting older and becoming more independent, I decided to look elsewhere. I'd done almost 10 years and I needed some adventure back in my life.

Risk Vs Reward

I left education because of the politics.

But this time, instead of leaving a career without a plan, I wrote an 'escape plan' of all the things I wanted to do with my life. The kids were growing up and opportunities were out there for the taking. When I left full time teaching, I took a part time role as a performance coach with WorldSkills UK, our national team of talented young apprentices that compete every other year in a 'Skills Olympics'. The WorldSkills movement raises the standard of industry globally with around 80 countries involved.

It was an honour to be selected; the role offered me a chance to use my skillset on a national level.

To top up my income I worked on site with my best mate and climbing buddy, Chris. Again, another close friend who had found me some work in the construction industry. The contrast from full time teaching to groundwork on a building site was like a breath of fresh air! Site work reminded me of simpler times, of digging trenches as a Marine, it was like therapy. A summer of this gave me the thinking space to revisit my escape plan.

Whilst looking for other opportunities, I answered a Facebook post from adventure filmmakers, Posing Productions. I was invited to provide support on a climbing film in Scotland.

That same day, director Al Lee called me to chat logistics and brief me up on kit. As soon as I put the phone down, I rang Chris. I started the conversation off with 'you're not going to believe what I'm up to next mate'. He laughed his head off and thought it was brilliant. We both loved Al's work and have been to several of his talks. He's a bit of a legend in the climbing world.

After the initial excitement of getting the opportunity, along came the apprehension. Here we go again!

I spent nine days as Al's right-hand man. The days were long and arduous, but we had an amazing time getting as much footage as we could. The small film crew were brilliant, and we were buzzing throughout the whole trip. Adrenaline is a powerful drug! The icing on the cake was that the film 'Stone Free', won best adrenaline film at Kendal Film Festival that year.

That trip was, without a doubt, the best adventure I'd been on since leaving the Corps. The cherry on top was that I supplied five of my original songs to be used on the film, the highlight of my musical journey so far.

I later went on to land a big contract training ex-offenders from Belmarsh Prison - another amazing experience that came about through my WorldSkills role.

I truly believe that the concepts of networking and reputation should be hammered into us when we are younger. Your network is everyone who you have direct contact with, social media, social circles and the like, your reputation is what people will say about you when you're not there. Both are extremely important factors that play a huge part in our wellbeing.

I also took work as an associate lecturer at the University of Derby. I specialised in behaviour management and assisted the education team in training and coaching trainee teachers on the PGCE course. It gave me huge insight and spurred me on to complete a degree in education.

I never thought I'd ever do a degree. Leaving school without any GCSEs can make you think it's unachievable, but I'd continued my education and never stopped learning after school. I understand motivation plays a huge part in accomplishing any goal, so I chose my modules carefully. I focused on wellbeing, motivation and behaviour, subjects that really appealed to me. I was fully invested. I was paying for it too and skint at the time, so I had to immerse myself in the process. The hard work paid off; I got a first-class honours.

Working outdoors was where I was happiest. The action movie industry had been on my escape plan too. I signed up to a military film agency a few years before starting Uni, doing bits of film work helped pay the bills and fill the fridge.

I landed roles on Kingsman one and Kingsman two, I played a CIA agent in one of Costner's films, ironically, I played an SBS operative in Stratton with Dominic Cooper, and I also spent a few days chasing Natalie Portman around a set. A far cry from delivering sandwiches for £3.50 an hour. It was all good fun, I got to work with some fantastic people and gained first-hand knowledge on how films are put together.

I developed my network further; I started to make and take more opportunities. I risked the comfort of a 9 to 5 income, and the psychological impact that countless rejections brought, but I learned to take them as lessons in resilience.

My reward is the amazing experiences that I had and the friends I made on that part of the journey.

How do you weigh up the risk versus the reward on your life journey?

Immediate Actions to Flourish

Looking back, I see that it could have gone either way for me, but the culmination of all my decisions, zero planning, and just winging my way through, gave me invaluable life experience and insights. Probably not the best way to do it, but always look for the learnings, accept your position and move forward.

I drew upon this hard-earned knowledge and experience to prepare for my 5 minute talk, sifting through what would be most useful and deciding the best way to present it.

I created a military-style crib card, with Immediate action drills to follow. These immediate action drills would be prompted by 3 overarching themes:

1. Be harder to kill
2. Be easier to love

3. Always fill your glass first

Be harder to kill is a reminder for us to work on our mental and physical health, to increase our resilience and help us to make clearer decisions.

The immediate actions I chose for this prompt are learn to breathe properly, stay hydrated, sleep well, eat well, and take up some form of physical training.

These basics are much more important than you think, and often overlooked.

Be easier to love reminds us that when we are in survival mode, we are hard to love. We put barriers up, we shut down and shrink our opportunities and we spread our woes! Maybe a bit of victim mentality going on there too. We need to learn to trust, to open our hearts and to be more human.

The immediate actions associated with this prompt are to develop your emotional intelligence, focus on improving the moment, practice gratitude, seek joy, and consider how to give by helping others where you can.

Understandably I left the Marines with little compassion, and didn't grasp the impact I had on others when I was angry and aggressive. I didn't even realise I was, it was the norm for me.

Always fill your glass first is the third prompt. When in survival mode we are least effective and rarely at our best. Working under pressure can be a good thing, but it's important to consider the long-term impact to your health and wellbeing.

Learning how to say "no" is a huge part of learning how to keep the glass topped up and I know how challenging this can be. Asking people for help when we are struggling is not only brave, but it's vital for our wellbeing.

I chose this prompt remembering that as my compassion returned, I went through a period of guilt and shame from past actions. I over-compensated and tried too hard to please everyone. I became self-conscious and struggled to make decisions. I felt too vulnerable to ask for help. I'd lost my agency, the feeling of having a good level of control over our life.

The two immediate actions I chose were, consider your intentions, and assert yourself with empathy.

In essence, learn to make decisions with authentic intent and, when communicating in high stress situations, try to understand the other person's position and state yours with clarity.

It's all too easy to turn to negative coping mechanisms when feeling low. Drinking, gambling, taking drugs, buying new things and blaming others, they're all responses that we know do not help in the long term. At best, they postpone or mask the issue; at worst they drive us deeper into emotional turmoil.

The idea behind the crib card was to remind the young me that there are other ways to cope and new skills yet to learn.

Develop A Growth Mindset

I developed the survive to flourish concept as a talk for a competition. But it became so much more than that. It became the starting point for a Lottery funded men's health group called the 'Leg Up' project. The crib card would prove to be an invaluable resource and had bullet pointed a clear self-development path for anyone to follow.

Working as a performance coach with WorldSkills UK had broadened my skillset, coaching centres on the development and guidance of the individual, we concentrated on marginal gains by identifying small changes to practice to achieve the best possible outcomes.

So, there was a shift from my previous teaching role.

Our wellbeing in everyday life can also be enhanced by looking for marginal gains and making minor, incremental changes to make large improvements over time.

It's one thing knowing what you need to do, but actioning it is a whole different challenge. This is where a look at the way we think becomes critical. Our mindset is what sets out the way we behave in challenging situations.

American psychologist, Dr Carol Dweck is a leading expert on mindset and identifies the difference between what she calls a 'growth' mindset and 'fixed' mindset.

With a fixed mindset we see no value in effort, we avoid challenge, give up at the first hurdle, and we are likely to criticise others and feel threatened by their success. We inhabit this way of thinking when we are in survival mode and are likely to see ourselves as a victim in all that happens to us.

When we adopt a growth mindset, we start to embrace problems, or challenges, with a belief that we can change, and we can learn from the hardships of life. Positive self-talk, the way we talk to ourselves, is a key component. To move forward we need to develop a growth mindset and reframe our internal dialogue with positive self-talk.

After all, if we don't learn to believe in ourselves, not only will we always be unhappy, but how can we expect others to believe in us?

Here's a few things to think about.

Acknowledge and embrace imperfections, and not just your own, everybody is different.

Stop seeking approval from others and learn to take criticism as a positive thing, no matter how harshly delivered.

Not all criticism is welcomed, but there is always something to learn from it. You may take onboard somebody else's opinion, or you may realise that they may not have your best interests at heart. It's not always easy to understand a person's true intentions.

Cultivate a sense of purpose to what you are trying to achieve and start to value your journey over the result that you seek. So many people think that achieving a huge goal will bring everlasting happiness - it doesn't - so enjoy the journey, enjoy each little daily win, and concentrate on the effort you put in, not the targets you tick off.

When problems arise, and they will, look for what you can learn from the situation, replace the word failing with the word learning. These challenges are an opportunity to grow, so identify when you are playing the victim and look for the lesson in amongst the hardship.

Don't just sit back and wait to be tested, take yourself out of your comfort zone on a regular basis to build your resilience before the inevitable challenge comes along. We never know when, and what difficulties await us, but we know there will be some so accept that this is a part of life.

Take ownership over your attitude, your mindset, the way you think, and remember to celebrate growth with others; that means enjoy their wins too. There is so much more joy in life when you can share and appreciate the little things.

Actively developing a growth mindset will change your life. Our reality is simply what we think.

Learn to Breathe Properly

Breathing properly optimises the body's systems and increases oxygen input, helping us to function to the very best of our ability. Poor breathing makes the heart work inefficiently, limiting our capacity to reason and reducing our stamina.

Tai chi taught me how to breathe properly. Becoming aware of and taking control of our breathing is something we can learn to do.

Developing this skill takes practise, but it will help us to identify when we are under stress.

We are not trying to avoid stress. Avoiding stress will only lower your ability to bounce back from future challenges. So, it's well worth planning some resilience training into your lifestyle. This will give you an opportunity to practise breathing techniques. Experiencing stress and learning to manage it effectively also builds confidence and self-belief.

When we push ourselves physically, we know It becomes harder to breathe, we sweat, and we become tired. But we are generally not taught how to remain calm when under psychological pressure.

Past traumas can trigger a fear response from the body, whether rational or not it will put the body into survival mode, and this is when learning to recognise and control our breathing comes into its own.

Practising correct breathing techniques can also help to reduce stress, manage anger, anxiety, and cravings. It can also help to manage pain and promote sleep improvement.

There are several different techniques we can use to breathe more effectively, but the basic procedure is simple: sit in a comfortable relaxed position, slowly inhale through the nose. Listen to the air going in and keep your shoulders relaxed.

Take note that your abdomen should expand, and your chest should only move slightly. If you study a baby breathing, you'll see that they do this naturally.

Exhale slowly through the mouth, purse your lips and pay attention to the slight 'whooshing' noise that you make. Just thirty seconds will make a noticeable difference to your state of mind.

Another technique is the 4-7-8 breathing method. First empty your lungs of air, then breathe in slowly through your nose for four seconds, filling up your lower abdomen. Hold the breath for seven seconds, and exhale through the mouth with your lips pursed for eight seconds. Try doing this twice a day, but only complete the cycle four times at most if you're new to this.

Sit or lie down when you practise this technique, as you may feel light-headed when you first start.

You could also try halving the time to 2-3-4 seconds instead. See what works best for you, there's no strict method to get the desired result.

These techniques can bring you to the present moment, reduce worry and help you to think with more clarity. For me, the main thing is that you become aware of your breathing; your 'conscious breath.' Learning yoga or tai chi will enhance this skill and add the element of physical training too, but if you have any major concerns about your respiratory system, make sure that you talk to your doctor first.

If we train ourselves to breathe as a method of dealing with stress, we are giving ourselves the best chance to make the right decisions under pressure. Find a technique that suits you and practise.

Stay Hydrated

By the time you feel thirsty, you are already dehydrated. Maintaining good fluid levels helps the heart and muscles work more efficiently. It helps to remove toxins, lubricate the joints, improves the digestive process and makes your skin look better. It will make you feel stronger, more alert, and reduce the possibility of mood swings, so it's worth making it your goal to stay topped up.

Recent research shows the effects of mild dehydration to be significant. Symptoms include feeling drowsy and sluggish, having lower attention levels, increased confusion and generally feeling low.

A research study on young adults reveals that drinking 300ml of water can boost cognitive performance by up to 25%. A bottle of water could be the one thing that keeps you alert on long road trips.

In the same study carried out by the University of Westminster, and the University of East London, a 31% improvement in attention for 7 to 9 year-olds was found after consuming only 25ml. This adds weight to my argument that children should be able to drink water in class at school. I'll leave that little gem there for the teachers amongst you to consider.

A general rule of thumb is to drink two litres of water a day, but we are all different. The easiest way to check how hydrated you are is to pay attention to the colour of your urine. The clearer it is, the more hydrated you are. Many people go through their lives continually dehydrated without ever knowing how much better they could feel. Will this incremental change make a big difference if you're not already doing it?

Yes, it will.

Try filling up a two-litre bottle of water in the morning and drinking it all before bedtime. Yep, simple. Make it into a habit and train yourself to become more conscious of how your fluid levels affect you. This is my go to immediate action if I'm feeling a bit flat.

It took me some time to get used to it, and I notice the difference in my state of mind when I forget to drink. If you don't like plain water, just add a bit of squash.

It is a well-known medical fact that our brain is made up of around 75% water and we need to keep it that way for it to work most effectively. If you want to perform at your best and feel better for it, hydration is a habit you need to get into.

And on the subject of forming positive new habits, it's worth thinking about dropping some bad habits too. What liquids are you consuming and are they harming or helping? Moderation on sugary drinks and alcohol is a must. Both are consumed for comfort.

Let's not kid ourselves when it comes to alcohol. It takes strength and courage to 'bat away' peer pressure or change your routine to help lower your intake. If alcohol is a weakness for you then keep track of what your intake is and take note of how you feel as a result of what you consume. If we can measure it, we can manage it! Only you know if it's a real problem, and you're the only one that can take control of that.

It costs next to nothing to take an old two-litre drinks bottle, fill it from the tap and keep it with you for the day. The hardest thing to do is form the habit.

Team up with a friend or family member and work as accountability partners. Send one another a picture of the full bottle in the morning and check in at the end of the day to show you have finished it. You can use an accountability partner for any area of personal development you choose to improve on.

It takes us an average of 66 days to form a new habit, so give it a go and don't give up easily.

I'll leave you with this. Aristotle is quoted to have said 'We are what we repeatedly do. Excellence, then, is not an act, but a habit'.

Eat Well

"We are what we eat" stated German philosopher Ludwig Feuerbach. That was back in 1848 in amidst the turmoil and stress of the German revolution. That's a lesson from history that's worth taking note of.

Keep it lean, keep it clean, and keep it green!

Different foods and drinks provide different amounts of energy. These are provided by the carbohydrates, protein and fats stored in those food sources. If we use more energy than we take on board, we lose weight. This is called calorie deficit. Eating well does not mean losing weight, that may be a goal you have, but the primary goal should be to optimise wellbeing over aesthetics.

Our diets are personal to us so you will need to find out what works best for you. This takes effort and time. Implement well informed changes you want to make, journal your findings, and make continual tweaks and improvements. It will be work in continual progress.

Consider the balance of carbs, protein and fat that you need for the lifestyle that you lead.

Adjust portion sizes and explore what works best for you. Keep a diary of how your diet makes you feel, as your body will benefit from avoiding certain foods. If you pay close attention to this, you will start to notice subtle differences.

Make sure you try new recipes and remember that no matter how hard you train, you cannot out train a poor diet. Eating healthy needs to be part of a lifestyle change, not just a temporary fix to get beach fit for a holiday.

When I focused on my diet, I found a renewed interest in cooking. Finding new recipes, better ingredients, and learning to enjoy the whole process of feeding myself and eating with family and friends. As my mum would say, 'a family that eats together stays together'. Yes, Mum, I know, I should have listened to you more.

Communal eating is something deep rooted within us. After all, feeding time is a vulnerable time for all animals. Being vulnerable together and sharing what we have openly would have been even more powerful back in our tribal history.

I think it's fair to say that the toughest part of eating well is cutting down on the bad stuff.

We eat because we are either hungry, or we do it for comfort. It's part of being a human being. I struggle with the latter when feeling low, but don't mind feeling hunger pangs on adventurous days out.

This little mantra helps me out, 'eat what you need, not what you want'. Remember small changes over time will get results, consistency will be the defining factor on this one though!

Writing a weekly menu works well for some, it can also save money. This may need the backing of your family, which could initially fill you with dread. But as with any team, work out something that motivates you all, get the 'buy in' from everyone in the house and be democratic. Work out responsibilities, have shared ownership and problem solve together!

Make it a challenge, not a problem. Be supportive and celebrate one another's culinary achievements.

Don't forget to observe how your diet makes you feel in terms of energy and mood and be aware that we are all different. There will be discomfort, but accept that this brings growth, so don't give up too easily on yourself.

If we inhabit the growth mindset we know that our efforts bring reward. That reward being, you feel much better, physically and mentally.

That person who has a body that you would die for may well be damaging their health to maintain that image. Sadly, this is a common problem.

If your diet is impacting on your health, mentally or physically, please seek medical advice from your doctor or a professional nutritionist.

But above all else, learn to love yourself whatever shape you're in and look after the only body that you will ever have.

Sleep Well

Lack of sleep poses a serious risk to your wellbeing. Long-term sleep deprivation will ruin your life. It affects your mood, your balance and your ability to concentrate which ultimately leads to poor decision-making and accidents. The immune system becomes ineffective, and we become prone to illness. In the long term, not getting enough sleep can raise your blood pressure and increase the risk of diabetes and heart disease.

So, getting a good night's kip is serious business.

Back in the military, we never took sleep seriously, it was part of the culture then. We used to say things like "I'll sleep when I'm dead" and you often heard "I only need three hours' sleep and I'm good to go."

Truth is we all need to get a certain amount of quality sleep to allow our bodies and our brains to rest and repair themselves.

In 2007 the World Health Organization classified night shift work as a probable carcinogen. This research finds a link between lack of sleep and cancer.

Poor sleep is also associated with an impaired ability to remember. If we want to maximise our ability to store new information, we need consistent quality sleep.

Where do we start? It's essential to sleep at regular times to improve the quality and quantity of your sleep. The body has a natural internal clock so you can establish and get used to a routine. If you have trouble going to bed at a reasonable time, getting some sunlight on your eyes as early in the morning as possible can help your body to re-establish its natural sleep pattern.

Make sure that your mattress is comfortable and that your bedroom is as peaceful as possible. To get to sleep, and maintain it, your body needs to be a couple of degrees cooler than in the day, around 18°C is said to be best for most people. You should also keep light and noise to a minimum.

Regular exercise can help relieve tension, but avoid vigorous exercise close to bedtime. Avoid caffeine in the hours before you sleep: try switching to herbal tea. Too much food or alcohol close to bedtime will cause broken sleep.

Alcohol may well get you to sleep, but it will cause you to wake up throughout the night, as will smoking, as Nicotine is a stimulant.

Avoid TV screens, using your laptop, and going on your mobile phone or tablet for as long as possible before bedtime.

Establishing a relaxing pre-bed routine can really help. You could plan some exercise early on in the evening and later on treat yourself to a relaxing hot bath and listen to some calming music, maybe light a scented candle? Once out of the tub do some gentle stretching and, before getting tucked up in bed, try some breathing and meditation techniques, or even listen to a sleep app. There you go, job done.

Remember that forming these positive routines will have a huge impact and can go a long way to putting your problems into perspective.

But, if you do find yourself lying wide awake, it might be worth getting up and doing something relaxing until you feel sleepy again because you want to avoid your body associating being awake with being in the bedroom.

Cortisol is our primary stress hormone. Our body produces it to stimulate us into action, and it is closely linked to the fight/flight response.

It also has several other functions that relate to keeping the body healthy. The levels of this hormone directly affect our sleep pattern, so it's imperative to manage stress as effectively as possible before we sleep.

If I'm struggling to shut off at night, I write down what's on my mind. In the cold light of day, I find that the issues plaguing me at 2am do not tend to be that big a deal. Tiredness muddles the mind. Writing my worries down helps me to prioritise my sleep and not spike cortisol levels.

And if you struggle to get a good night's sleep no matter how hard you try, then you need to visit your doctor and discuss it further.

But be advised, prescription sleeping pills may help in the short term, but they're not going to give you the quality of sleep that you need for your immune system to do its job properly. To find out more on this subject, research restorative sleep theory.

Sleep is your best friend. It's one of the most important aspects of your life that you need to master. Practice is key, so try different routines, monitor what works best for you, and don't stop trying new strategies until it becomes the norm to sleep well.

Physical Training

Exercise not only maintains physical fitness, but also helps us to stay mentally healthy. Current UK guidelines for adults state that we should do at least 150 minutes of moderate aerobic activity per week, and on top of that, strength exercises on two or more days a week to target all the major muscle groups. It's worth including daily stretches for maximum benefit too. Remember, these guidelines are the minimum recommended. If you are planning on making big physical changes, I would advise you to enlist the support of a good physical training instructor to maintain motivation and minimise the risk of injury.

Research from clinical professor of psychiatry, Dr John J. Ratey, strongly suggests that exercise prepares the brain for taking on and storing information. He states that "in addition to priming our state of mind, exercise influences learning directly, at the cellular level, improving the brain's potential to log in and process new information." So, if you're studying or need to stay on top of a mentally taxing job, it makes sense to ensure you're getting enough exercise.

Along with eating well and sleeping well, exercise is a major component to raising your level of wellbeing.

The only investment you will need to make is time and effort; if you get creative you don't need to subscribe to a gym to achieve good results. But if you do find joining a gym or club helpful for motivation, then go for it.

We're all different. What works best for me is outdoor adventure training, because it challenges me both mentally and physically. The health benefits of green space are also well-documented and exploring the outdoors can be a great way to enhance your overall wellbeing. It keeps exercise interesting, and it gives us a reason to get outside, find new places, and meet new people. This still plays a massive part for me in my personal journey. A good walk is my go-to when I'm feeling a bit low, and we all get days like that.

Twenty five minutes of brisk walking a day is moderate aerobic activity. Alternatively, 75 minutes of vigorous aerobic activity, such as running or walking with a weighted backpack, is a good baseline for exercise each week.

Start light and build yourself up at a realistic pace that suits you, listen to your body, but don't make excuses for every little ache and discomfort you feel. You will need to break through some discomfort to grow. Little often is the way to start. Set yourself a daily discomfort and aim to make that the norm. Get comfortable with being uncomfortable.

Strength exercises can be done anywhere using a bodywork programme. There's lots to choose from and a quick internet search will give you plenty of ideas.

These guidelines are the minimum that you should be doing, but once you get into exercising, you'll be surprised at how much better it will make you feel.

To keep you on track there's fitness trackers such as a Fitbit, Garmin, or Strava. These are great for motivation because they can help you track your progress and find training partners. It's a good idea to establish a routine too.

I find working with several training partners across different disciplines keeps me interested, and there's a level of accountability as you don't want to let them down. This is great for when you're just not feeling it, because that little bit of peer pressure is enough to get you off the sofa, and we always feel better after a training session.

However much or little exercise you can manage, getting started is the main thing. Human beings are designed to move, and we feel very much better for it.

Why not just pick a charity that you support, get out there and do a Couch To 5k with some friends? Keep it simple, but get started sooner rather than later.

Be Easier to Love

Being harder to kill is all about drilling down on the basics, breathing properly, drinking plenty of water, eating well, sleeping well and staying physically fit. When I left the Marines, I had all the tools I needed to work on my physical fitness, even if I was injured, but my biggest struggle was to understand myself and that it was my attitude, my mindset, that was holding me back.

I lacked empathy and projected my anger and frustration under stressful situations, or when drunk. Eventually I would experience low self-esteem as friends took a step back or sniped at me from a safe distance. Every time I seemed to be doing ok somebody would damage my car.

It was clearly someone in my circle. I hadn't yet worked out that not all friends, I use the term loosely, want to see you do well. In the wise words of a good friend Bobby, jealousy surrounds us!

I struggled on and off with poor mental health for several years and did my best to mask how I felt. I was ashamed to feel that way, at the time it made me feel weak.

I'd been out of the military for five years when I landed my teaching role. I still felt a bit 'disconnected' and I was reading lots of self-help books. I wanted to get my head around how I was feeling. My knee was in better shape, I was getting my fitness back up to speed, and I was looking after myself.

Being physically fitter was great, but I needed to be easier to love, and this would take more time to develop as my view on life had been skewed from being in the Marines. My attitude needed adjusting. It's hard to undo all that.

Having decided that be easier to love would be my second prompt, I chose the immediate actions that helped me to achieve this.

Develop emotional intelligence, improve the moment, practise gratitude, seek joy and learn how to give, these are what I identified as helping me the most. These all stemmed from a combination of my professional development at work and learning the mental and physical discipline of tai chi.

Both played a huge part in my life and made me consider who I really was and how I was treating others.

Put simply, emotional intelligence is our capacity to understand, control and express our emotions, and to handle interpersonal relationships with empathy and care. High emotional intelligence has been described as the key to a successful personal and professional life, but for me it was simply about becoming happier.

Goleman suggests that there's four fundamental parts to emotional intelligence: self-awareness, self-management, social awareness (empathy) and relationship management.

Developing our emotional intelligence is always work in progress, but to get you started, here's four simple questions to ponder.

Mark yourself out of 10 for each question; note anything below 5 as an area for development.

1) How aware are you of your own feelings?
2) How well do you manage your emotions in times of stress?
3) How well do you understand other people's feelings?
4) How confident are you when you meet new people?

You may also ask a trusted friend or family member their thoughts about you based on these questions. You will get even more of an insight into any 'blind spots' you may have.

That is, actions or behaviours that others see in you, but you are unaware of.

You might not agree with their opinion, and it might be uncomfortable, but view it as a chance to grow. An open and honest discussion will be of the most benefit.

Remember that useful negative feedback is extremely valuable, so develop your ability to identify, and learn from, constructive criticism.

Being easier to love will mean you have to learn to let certain things go and accept that some situations are simply out of your control.

Self-Awareness and Self-Management

Emotional Self-awareness is our ability to understand our emotions and the impact that they have on our actions. Improving this will help us make more informed decisions and better choices. Learning tai chi gave me the emotional space to consider what thoughts were consuming my mind. I soon realised that I was spending most of my time worrying about things that hadn't happened and agonising over past mistakes.

I started to find strategies to live in the moment and to be more emotionally balanced, and I learned how to give my head a break. Walking helped me to think clearly, and I started to feel happier the more I understood myself.

Self-reflective practice at work helped me too. During teacher training I was asked to identify my areas of strength and weaknesses, and to look for opportunities and the threats that might stand in the way of me becoming the best teacher that I could be.

This is known as a SWOT analysis; it's commonly used in business and is a great tool that can be used from an individual perspective. Such as, to help you develop a skill, identify a problem, write a CV, or even to set up your own business.

I also took psychometric tests that made me consider my personality traits and natural areas of strength. I found the Clifton strength finder to be an insightful and useful tool. Give it a google if this sort of thing interests you.

During teacher training we did peer observations with one another, and I journaled my progress, setting myself goals on the way.

Self-reflective practice is a continual process; it can be uncomfortable at first, but the more we do it the more natural it feels. We adapt and we change. You can become more self-aware by keeping a diary, asking trusted friends to describe you, setting yourself some goals, and regularly taking an honest look at your progress.

Self-management is being able to handle our emotions effectively in distressing or exciting situations, and this is a game changer.

I'd obviously done a fair bit of overcoming fear and excitement as a Marine - I had that bit nailed - but I didn't gain any transferable skills to help me sort out my more complex feelings. I realise now that my frontal lobes, the reasoning part of my brain, were still in development, so I didn't have the hardware or knowledge to process what I'd experienced.

It became easier to self-manage emotions the more I came to learn who I was and what made me tick, but there's more to it than that. Taking ownership of what you do is essential, especially if you want to get ahead at work or keep your personal life on track. Accountability, showing initiative and being organised are all key self-management skills. These are all areas that we can develop if we choose to.

Working on yourself, mentally, is not easy work. It can become confusing, frustrating and at times you will feel disappointed by past mistakes. But they are the nuggets of hardship you have already obtained, they are what prepare you for future challenges. Try to remember that there is no final destination to reach when we work on our mindset. Learning is a lifelong process to be enjoyed, not endured.

Empathy

Social awareness, or empathy, is our capacity to understand and share what others are feeling. This was not something I thought about much in the Marines, it just wasn't on the radar.

Veterans can easily come across as harsh or coarse, but they are just used to talking to each other bluntly. Male dominated industries, such as construction, don't tend to be areas where you develop what we call 'soft skills' either. This probably relates to the fact that men do not want to be perceived as being weak, especially in an industry that has a culture of piss taking and pushing buttons. It's not all with malice, but like the military, the building game is not a place of empathy.

As I left the forces, I still cared about people, but I know that I was very outspoken and tactless. I got straight to the point. I was also trying – and failing – to manage the transition back into civilian life and this is where I found out that drink and drugs, as coping mechanisms, just lead to drama.

The 3 Ds of doom. Drama, in the sense that I'd perceive my issues to be worse than they were, and I perpetuated this by creating new problems to solve from poor decision making. Also getting drawn into other people's problems was an issue for me, like some sort of hero complex!

It was a steep learning curve. I upset quite a few people, and I'll just park that there for now...

We can develop our empathy by developing our curiosity when meeting new people. Not trying to sound creepy, but humans have a natural inquisitiveness, we just seem to lose it growing up. Any parents out there know that children ask all the awkward questions! Curiosity is a human trait.

However, historian Studs Terkel would say 'Don't be an examiner, be the interested enquirer.'

So, don't just go out and interrogate the old lady at the bus stop that you've never met. Genuinely asking her how she's doing is a nice place to start.

So, challenge your previous beliefs, preconceptions and prejudices, keep an open mind about others and look for similarities rather than differences.

We are all human beings! Let's celebrate our differences, I mean without them how interesting would life be?

Actively listen to people too. This means put your agenda on hold and fully engage with the person who is speaking to you.

How often have you found yourself drifting off or preparing your reply before they've even finished? By the same token, you've probably noted this happening when you're trying to get your point across.

As well as listening with intent, we should try to be more open and honest with others. Being vulnerable takes courage, but mutual understanding relies upon us to share our deepest thoughts and feelings, our true beliefs.

Every time you listen to somebody, listen as though you are going to learn something from them, and you probably will.

By exercising emotional empathy, we apparently mirror the activity of neurons in the other person's brain to experience what they are feeling. Another human trait.

The downside to emotional empathy is that it can become overwhelming, and some people are highly sensitive to others' feelings.

But empathy is not to be confused with sympathy. We used to have a saying in the Corps, "if you want sympathy look it up in the dictionary, it's between shit and syphilis'.

Harsh I know, but I find myself using this saying when discussing the difference between the two.

For me, sympathy is more aligned to feelings of sorrow or pity for someone's misfortunes, and I don't believe that is useful to anyone when giving assistance or support.

Developing your empathy can be as simple as taking time to consider other people's feelings and how your behaviour impacts upon them.

When we practise empathy, it soon becomes clear that everyone is dealing with their emotions differently: it's part of being human.

Before you pre-judge anybody, take a few seconds to consider that they may be struggling.

Think before you say something stupid: words cannot be unsaid. And above all, remember that kindness is king when sincere and with good intention.

Relationship Management

Relationship management is such a major part of our lives because unless we shut ourselves away and become a hermit, we have no choice but to interact and build interpersonal relationships.

For many it's complex and complicated, as to varying degrees most relationships are in a state of flux. If you are on a personal journey of self-development, expect a little more turbulence than usual and I can guarantee there will be at least one person that makes a huge drama out of it.

It's worth communicating your intentions to those close to you. This may alleviate their uncertainty as you develop, grow and work towards personal achievements. Your behaviours and mindset will change, and it will be challenging. Just remember to consider the bigger picture.

There is no doubt in my mind that we expose insecurities in others when we start to shine and feel good, unfortunately there's not a lot you can do about it. That was a tough lesson for me to learn and it made me observe who was sharing my wins with me and who was talking me down.

Either way, we change, we grow, we learn, we make mistakes, we learn more. It's just the way it is, but becoming more effective at managing relationships will be the key that unlocks the door to a happier life.

Our level of self-awareness, self-management and empathy all come into play. Adopt a 'kaizen' approach to improving your emotional intelligence. We are all work in progress, but we can always aim for continuous improvement.

Kaizen is a Japanese word, and although it has several meanings depending on context, I'm going to use this one. Kai meaning change and zen meaning good, so basically changing for the better.

During my dark days, I just needed to re-programme my head to where I was rather than where I had been. I needed to better understand my environment and listen more, and when I eventually did, life got easier in every area: friendships, my teaching skills at work, how I viewed myself, how I networked with new people and how I made decisions.

Helping others is a great way to improve our emotional intelligence, and even though it seems like the last thing we want to do when we feel down, giving yourself a different perspective on life is good for personal growth.

Studies have shown that anti-social behaviour falls by as much as 10% when school children actively participate in programmes to develop emotional intelligence. Significant improvements were also observed in their enjoyment of school, their behaviour, their learning skills, and their academic achievements.

For me, understanding how our survival instincts can trigger unwanted behaviour was mind blowing, especially when we look at emotional hijacking, mentioned previously. We can't avoid being triggered by someone else's words or actions, and it's not always done intentionally on their part, or ours, but It's crazy to think that our heart rate can rise by as many as 20 beats per minute from one beat to the next. Our body literally gets hijacked into red-line survival mode and we say and do things that we later regret.

Becoming aware of this and training to breathe through it made a big difference to me.

Just being self-aware, and using strategies to remain as calm as possible, can give you a chance to try and improve the moment as best you can.

Remember: high emotional intelligence has been described as the key to a successful personal and professional life, the way we manage our relationships with those around us lays at the heart of this.

Improve the Moment, Practise Gratitude, Seek Joy

Whilst on a conflict management training course I revisited the concept of improving the moment, which relates to being present, or being in the now. Several years before, Tai chi had helped me to understand how important this was, and I learned that applying the principle to heated situations can help avoid unnecessary escalation. Granted, it's easier said than done.

If you can focus on improving the moment when faced with a non-physical threat, then there's a good chance you can de-escalate the situation.

If I find myself caught up in confrontation, I attempt to 'observe myself' and become aware of my emotional state in order to influence what action to take next. This can sometimes be referred to as the 'detached witness' where you almost feel as though you are in a film.

I make an effort to relax my facial expression and body language. I slow my breathing and attempt to consider the other person's position. I assume they might be having a bad day, and that I'm not the root of their anger, even if it is being directed at me. It's a technique that has worked for me in many situations.

When I'm struggling with negative thoughts, I practise gratitude. I count my blessings, and I work on keeping a positive frame of mind. I also think about whether I need to drink more water, get something to eat or get some sleep.

Whatever stress you're experiencing, just reminding yourself to improve the moment can be a great start. It can change everything.

Like all changes that we hope to make to improve our lives, learning to be grateful for what we have will take time and practice.

Gratitude is a very powerful emotion, and there's plenty of ways to practise it. Consider those less fortunate.

Military life was a no frills affair and it taught me to be grateful for the comforts at home.

I still live a simple life and remind myself that I have the basics that some people don't. If I can fill the fridge and pay the bills, I'm all good.

I'm clothed and warm, I have shelter and I have loved ones around me. So, there's plenty for me to be grateful for.

Telling others how much you appreciate them is literally priceless: it costs nothing, but it can mean so much to someone. That may be the trigger that helps them through a bad time. Showing one another gratitude makes us feel like we belong, it connects us.

Joy is also a powerful, positive emotion evoked by wellbeing, success, good fortune, and helping others. Watching someone you love overcome adversity and achieve great things can bring a huge amount of joy, as can watching the sun rise over the sea with the right company. I guess it depends entirely on your perception, but if you practise gratitude, joy is likely to follow.

I walked myself back to fitness out in the countryside. It made me happy, and I started to look at things differently. The trees, the plants, the wildlife. All the different smells. The wind and rain in my face. I started to appreciate more about what I had and worried less about what I didn't have.

Exploring nature and the environment around us can bring a deep sense of happiness and pleasure. Connect with the outdoors more, be kinder to people just because you can, and shift your focus from what others have. After all, you really don't know what's going on in their world.

Here's a mini recap, teacher style:

When you find yourself in a difficult situation, focus on the best possible outcome.

Every morning, write down five things that you are grateful for and why.

Each day, make it your mission to do at least one act of kindness. Say hello to a stranger and smile, open a door for somebody or ask how you can help if someone looks unsure.

Please don't be offended if they don't appreciate the gesture though, who knows what they are dealing with, they might be deep in survival mode?

Learning to Give

At our worst times, all we want to do is shut the door and shut the world out. I call it getting in the trench. But this is the time when you need to strike out, meet new people, and maintain strong friendships.

On the road to a better life, be aware that our time is the most precious commodity that we have. No matter how much money we stack up, we can't buy time back. But for me, it's quality that truly counts and offering time to help others will change your whole outlook on life.

Volunteering not only connects you socially, but it can also open up career opportunities and help you learn new skills.

When I got myself back on track mentally, physically and financially, I volunteered for the local Search and Rescue Team. I learnt some incredible new skills and I met some fantastic people. Helping others in their time of need gave me a fulfilled sense of purpose and put my own troubles into perspective.

One of the team I connected with was Stu.

Whilst going through his own personal hardships one Christmas, he decided to get out and help the homeless. Stu then set out to change his life by doing what he called '52 acts of random kindness'. This entailed helping a stranger at least once a week for a whole year. This journey led him to join the search and rescue team.

He didn't stop there; he used the medic training we received to be a community responder and from that experience went on to give support to medical teams out in Africa. All voluntary.

Giving your time can be immensely rewarding. It can reduce personal stress and boost emotional intelligence by connecting you with others.

It breaks down social and cultural barriers, it brings meaning to your life as you contribute positively to social change.

As a young teenager, I volunteered to work in a care home for the elderly, as part of my Duke of Edinburgh award. I was a bit nervous before I went in, but I made lots of new friends. They were fascinating to listen to, and I learned a lot about the area that I grew up in. Looking back, I think that's where my interest in local history was sparked. This would be something that got me out of the house exploring Charnwood Forest on darker days to come.

Research has shown that volunteering can add up to five years on to your life expectancy, providing you do it with good intentions, because volunteering for personal gain alone weakens the positive effects.

When times are getting tough, we tend to shut down little by little as our self-esteem takes a hit. This can creep up on us and before we know it we don't want to leave the house, and we're back in the trench.

At the point when you don't want to talk to anybody about your troubles, ask yourself what you can do for others. And be honest, could it be that you might just be feeling sorry for yourself?

We all inhabit the victim mentality from time to time, I think it's quite common, but it doesn't help us to dwell in this state.

Opening your heart and helping others is a sure-

fire way to give you a sense of purpose and put your problems into perspective.

Why not get out there and give some of your time to those who will really appreciate it?

You'll be surprised at who you meet, what you learn, and how it makes you feel.

Consider Your Intentions

If we set out with only our personal gain in mind, I am convinced that it's only a matter of time before we live to regret our choices. Bad intention always comes back round to bite us on the arse, and the longer it takes to learn this lesson, the harder the lesson becomes.

Consider your intentions is the first immediate action that I chose for 'Always fill your glass first'.

I remember my compassion returning and bringing with it a boat load of emotions that I'd never experienced before. I started struggling to make decisions that involved even the smallest conflict.

I ended up trying to please everyone and worried about upsetting people. At work, I struggled to say no, I took on too much and became run down and frustrated. This put me into survival mode where anger and aggression would resurface, and I would push the people that cared for me away just to get some headspace.

I burnt out within the first two years of my teaching career, which is very common. I had failed to fill my own glass. I was eager to please at work, and at home I was desperately trying to salvage a relationship that, in reality, had already failed. And I desperately missed my first born who had moved away with her mum.

It would take me some time to understand and accept my part in both break ups, but we live, and we learn, and some of the most difficult lessons serve us well in the future.

When I started to make decisions based on good intentions, my life changed dramatically. I hadn't been self-aware enough to understand that I was just acting mainly on impulse. The chimp was in control.

I was approaching tough decisions by scrutinising as many possible worst-case scenarios that I could think of. It was obviously influenced from my time in the Corps, but the thing is we are all hard wired to look for the negative. Thinking like this all the time had drained me.

Considering our intentions is a shift to becoming more self-aware; taking some time to set clear and positive intentions will pay dividends. If something that we attempt falls short of our expectations, or if we upset somebody, we could forgive ourselves more easily if we used good unselfish reasoning from the outset. We are only human, and we all screw up, but acting from a place of authentic intent will lead to a happier existence and less regret.

We can also consider the intentions of others and there's nothing wrong with asking someone a well-meaning question. Unquestioned assumptions lead us down a dark path. I know it takes courage to ask the questions that you might not want to know the answer to, but if you want to get your head straight, you must.

The younger me knowingly manipulated situations for personal gain without empathy, but it doesn't work out well in the long term. It might be a useful exercise to take a few minutes to reflect on a moment where you were thinking only about what you had to gain?

Be brutally honest with yourself. How did that work out for you? And how do you feel about it now?

These days, before I make an important decision, I think to myself, “Am I doing this for the right reasons for everybody involved?”

When faced with tough decisions it pays to take a ‘time out’, be totally honest with yourself, and consider your intentions.

Assert Yourself with Empathy

The final immediate action that I chose would be assert yourself with empathy. This requires a high level of self-awareness and is a skill that we should aim to develop.

We know it's not possible to go through life getting everything our own way, but there are times when we feel we are always the one who must compromise. At work, at home, in a relationship, or even if you find yourself in a disagreement with a stranger.

Learning to stick up for yourself, to say no, or to ask for help can be very difficult for some, and being able to set clear boundaries is important for your wellbeing.

There are those who have no problem asking for what they want. They are assertive, but some may be using aggression to lever their position. Many will not even realise that they are being bullish in their approach.

Before the lessons started to get tougher for me, I was pushy and aggressive, I didn't realise I was doing it, it had become my norm.

I had no idea how much of a negative impact this was having on my life until it was too late. Forcing your issues on to other people is common, and it only adds pressure and stress to an already stressful situation. Projection is a term worth mentioning too. This is when we unconsciously push our unwanted traits or emotions onto someone else, and I know I've done this without realising it in the past. It's more common than you think, it's very destructive, and very confusing. This is what made considering intentions, being open, and being honest, such big parts in unscrambling my scrambled head.

When you start to assert yourself with empathy, you are saying 'I care about you, but I also care about myself'. Try to understand their position and assert yours with clarity.

This may be easier said than done. It takes humility, courage, patience, and self-confidence to consider other people's feelings first before we steam in with our own wants and needs.

I guess it all depends upon the circumstances you find yourself in, but for me, it's the only way to navigate through avoidable drama.

You will need to learn to set clear boundaries, and this will take courage. Professor of philosophy and a leading researcher in social work, Brené Brown, says "choose discomfort over resentment". This is her go to mantra when she needs to make a decision that will impact upon her wellbeing.

Asserting yourself with empathy is about aiming for the win-win in difficult interpersonal circumstances. It's about communicating your intentions, actively listening, explaining your reasoning when you need to, and keeping others in the picture with how you wish to live your life.

I get that we all meet, or have, people in our lives that have no interest in our wellbeing and they're only out for themselves. They feed off negative energy, enjoy upsetting people, and love to get the upper hand by triggering for control.

Conflict arises when one person's needs are not being met by another. If their need is to over-power you to feel in control then you will never meet their needs unless you give up your position. Nobody will flourish in a situation like this.

Learning to assert yourself with empathy is not about them, it's about you maintaining self-esteem and knowing that you've approached conflict to the best of your ability.

Begin with the End in Mind

We'll never please everyone we meet, we shouldn't try too hard to either, but I think we owe it to ourselves to have the best life possible.

What does that mean to me? I need to know that if my life ended tomorrow, I would be happy with what I've achieved. Or if I was told I only had several months to live, I would feel that I've got my house in order, so to speak. No regrets, nothing left to say that needed to be said, and nothing left to achieve that I wasn't already working on, time permitted that is.

We can do anything we want to, within reason, but we can't do everything!

I've shared the best of what helped me on my route back to a happier life, and I will continue to apply this knowledge daily.

I still have dark days, like everyone else, I deal with events that are completely out of my hands, the uncontrollable. But I truly hope that some of the things I've shared help you.

It's not easy to change our mindset and behaviour. Our will power is less likely to work than building solid routines. So, practise the simpler tasks mentioned, like learning to breathe, staying hydrated, eating better, improving your sleep and ensuring that you move your body more.

Movement creates motivation to change. Effort will bring results. Happiness does not come easy for everyone, but everyone can learn to control the controllable.

And let's acknowledge that you can't expect to flourish all the time. Let's also remember that dark times pass if we don't wallow in our own self-pity. We have more ability to control the way we think than we realise.

And what's the alternative?

Are you just going to let life happen to you?

Or is it time to take control of the controllable?

Look for the growth in hardship, see problems as a challenge, not a threat, and set some goals to move forward with your life in a positive way.

Where do I begin? I hear you say.

Begin with the end in mind, but instead of a physical destination, or a dream goal, have a think about how well you know yourself, and if your future self will thank you for your current choices.

If success is peace of mind, understanding yourself should be a top priority. After all, your life is the culmination of every moment you experience and this is your journey to enjoy and endure.

I will leave you with one last thought, in memory of my dad. "it's nice to be important, but it's more important to be nice".

I wish you all the best on your journey, and remember, kindness is King.

Bibliography

Bennett, B. (2003) *Emotional yoga*. Kent: Bantam

Carr, A. (2011) *Positive Psychology: The Science of Happiness and Human Strengths.* 2nd Edition. London: Routledge

Cherkowski, S., and Walker, K. (2014) 'Flourishing communities: re-storying educational leadership using a positive research lens'. *International Journal of Leadership in Education,* 17(2) pp. 200-216

Dix, P. (2010) *The Essential Guide to Taking Care of Behaviour.* 2nd edition. Harlow: Pearson

Dweck, C. (2012) *Mindset: How you can fulfil your potential.* London: Constable and Robinson

Goleman, D. (1995) *Emotional Intelligence.* London; Bloomsbury

Hefferon, K., and Boniwell, I. (2011) *POSITIVE PSYCHOLOGY: Theory, Research and Applications*, Maidenhead: Open University Press

Kahneman, D. (2012) *Thinking, Fast and Slow.* London: Penguin books

Merzel, D.G. (2001) *24/7 Dharma: Impermanence, No-Self, Nirvana.* Boston: Journey Editions

Millman, D. (2000) *Living on Purpose: Straight Answers to Life's Tough Questions.*, Novato, California: New World Library

Mitchell, S. (1988) *Tao Te Ching.* London: Macmillan

Ody, P., Lyon, C., and Vilinac, D. (2000) *The Chinese Herbal Cookbook: Healing foods from East and West.* London: Kyle Cathie Limited

Peter, S. (2012) *The Chimp Paradox.* London: Vermillion

Peterson, C., Park, N., and Seligman, M.E.P. (2005) 'ORIENTATIONS TO HAPPINESS AND LIFE SATISFACTION: THE FULL LIFE VERSUS THE EMPTY LIFE' *Journal of Happiness Studies*, 6 pp. 25-41

Ratey,J.J. and Hagerman, E. (2010) *SPARK! How exercise will improve the performance of your brain.* London: Quercus

Ryan, R.M. and Deci, E.L. (2000) 'Self-Determination Theory and the Facilitation of Intrinsic Motivation, Social Development, and Well-Being', *The American Psychologist,* 55(1) pp.68-78

Seligman, M.E.P. and Csikszentmihalyi, M. (2000) 'Positive Psychology: An Introduction', *American Psychologist,* 55(1) pp. 5–14

Seligman, M.E.P. (2011) *Flourish: A new understanding of Happiness and Well-being* London: Nicholas Brearley Publishing

Syed, M. (2011) *Bounce: The myth of talent and the power of practice.* London: Fourth Estate

Van Der Kolk, B. (2015) *The Body Keeps the Score: Mind, Brain and Body in the Transformation of Trauma.* London: Penguin books

Wilhelm, R. (2003) *I Ching or Book of changes.* London: Penguin books

Printed in Great Britain
by Amazon

11633009R00078